Jubilant Whispers

and
Other Melodic Lyrics

by *Michael H. Hanson*

An Imprint of Copper Dog Publishing, LLC

Jubilant Whispers and other Melodic Lyrics

by Michael H. Hanson

Copyright ©2017 Copper Dog Publishing, LLC
All rights reserved. No part of this book may be reproduced in any manner whatsoever without prior written permission from the publisher, except where noted in the text and in the case of brief quotations embodied in critical articles and reviews.

Published by Racket River Press, an Imprint of Copper Dog Publishing, LLC
537 Leader Circle, Louisville, CO 80027
Visit our Web site: www.copperdogpublishing.com

Credits:
Cover and Interior Design: Helen H. Harrison
Written by Michael H. Hanson
Cover art: iStockPhoto

Library of Congress Control Number (PCN) applied for.
ISBN: 978-1-943690-19-0 Print
ISBN: 978-1-943690-21-3 Kindle

Second Edition December 2017
First Edition: 2010
Printed in the United States of America

Dedication

*for
Helen, Keith, Wayne, and Cynthia,
my Sisters and Brothers*

Acknowledgements

It is the supreme art of the teacher to awaken joy in creative expression and knowledge.

— Albert Einstein

With fond gratitude I remember Massena Central High School English Teachers: Thomas Maxcy, Josephine MacKenzie, and Sandra Long for that long ago active encouragement of my nascent teen writing skills; and S.U. Newhouse College Professors: Dr. Stanley Alten, Dr. Sharon Hollenback, and Prof. Richard L. Bryer for teaching me that the pursuit of excellence must be tempered with professionalism, discipline, and focus.

With the deepest appreciation I thank you all.

Michael H. Hanson
Piscataway, NJ
Autumn 2017

Table of Contents

CHAPTER ONE
Romance 13

    A SONG 15
    CRYPTICALLY HIP 16
    ON A GOLDEN SHORE* 17
    ON ERRANT DAYS 19
    CONQUEROR KISS (SHE SAID) 20
    REMEMBER 21
    HARBOR DECK 22
    FIRST KISS 23
    CHANCE MET IN MARYLAND 24
    SUMMER'S END 25
    CANDY GIRL 26
    A MEAL 27
    FIRST TRYST 28
    AUTUMN'S KISS 29
    VALENTINE 30
    RAIN 31
    FIRST LOVE 32
    STRANGERS WITH NAMES 33
    PEN PALS 34
    UNREQUITED 35
    LAST TIME 36
    AN EVENING SHORE 37
    THE BREAD OF HER SMILE 38
    I REMEMBER HER KISS 39
    PERHAPS ONE DAY 40
    SUPERCOLLIDER 41

CHAPTER TWO
Introspection 43

    JUBILANT WHISPERS 44
    HAUNTED 45
    FADING 46
    FORWARD 47
    I WANTED 48
    I GUESS 50
    IS IT? 51
    LIFELINE 52
    DREAMS AND FATES 53
    ELEGIAC APPAREL 54
    BROTHER'S CHILD 55
    FRAGMENTING 56
    GOODBYE 57
    IF I 58
    WHAT SHE SEES 59
    IN SLEEP 60
    DOES ANYBODY 61
    ADRIFT 62
    HOMUNCULUS 63
    KING MIDAS'S BROTHER 64
    GENESIS 65
    NO LONGER 66
    WITHIN MY HEART 67

CHAPTER THREE
The Past 69

    WHEN I WAS SMALL 70
    NUMB 72
    FAMILY 75
    WHEN MY BROTHER WAS PSYCHIC 76
    WOOD MOSAIC 79
    REPAIRMAN 80

Chapter Four
Nature 81

Solitary Spring 82
Spring Blossoms 83
August Breathes 84
This Wintertide 85

Chapter Five
Beauty 87

Naked in Waves 88
Chocolate Dancer 89
This Maryland 90
Into Colors 93
Walls 94

Chapter Six
Whimsy 95

The Poet Store 96
Ego Pricing 97
The Phelpsian Age 98
A Poem 99

Chapter Seven
Between Days 101

Cusp of December 103
Autumn Aches 104
The House Of Doze 105
End 106
The Waves of Jubilee 107
Before Thanksgiving 108
Suspended 109
Such Reverence 110
Sweet November 111
November's Mist 112

Cloaked In Autumn	113
Out Of Phase	114
Any Belief	115
Into Autumn's Heart	116
The African Dream	117
Raising This Light	118
Are There Answers?	119
The Vernis Layer	120
Spicy Juice	121
Happy Today	122
Earth And Rain	123
A Sword	124
The Secret Rhyme	125
Two Flowers	126
Unbroken	127
Summer Angel	128
Lightning's Blink	129
September's Sauce	130
Summer Leaves	131
After The Burglary	132
'Neath Shadow Bars	133

Introduction

Seven years later and I have come full circle. "Jubilant Whispers", first published in 2010, was originally my second collection of poetry, printed by a different press than my first anthology, "Autumn Blush," and marking an important milestone in my poetic life, i.e., that my first book wasn't a once-in-a-lifetime aberration, but merely the beginning of what I hope will be a nice sizable collection of poetry books that I will create over the rest of my life. As with "Blush", "Whispers" has been out of print for several years, and like my first anthology it is now being reprinted by Racket River Press, an imprint of Copper Dog Publishing LLC.

And what difference does seven years make? Quite a bit if you really want to know. As I recently did with "Blush" I have gone through and re-edited every single poem in this current collection, rewriting the odd line and/or end-rhyme, thus making these tighter and hopefully better reads.

I removed five of the darkest poems from this book and reprinted them in my horror poetry anthology, "Dark Parchments: Midnight Curses and Verses" published by Moondream Press in 2015, and thus needed to replace them with five new works I created over the past year.

Another poem was removed to be part of a future collection of Science Fiction and Fantasy poems I have put together, tentatively titled "Android Girl: And Other Sentient Speculations" which I hope makes it to print by 2018, and that poem was also replaced with one of my newer works.

Also, unlike the first edition of Jubilant Whispers, I have grouped all of these poems into chapters that more clearly define and regiment their tone, mood, and vision, a decidedly different experience than the free-for-all mix that was the paradigm of the earlier edition.

Then, less than one month before publication, the publisher requested that an additional thirty-one unpublished poems be added to this second edition as a bonus gift to the readers.

Last but not least I have added a subtitle to help identify this as a different animal from its similarly titled forebear.

I hope you enjoy this cornucopia of dreams, hopes, worries, wants, and fears. They only truly come to life when read by you… and don't be shy about re-gifting this anthology to loved ones, family, and friends. Poetry is a blessing meant to be shared.

Embrace your dreams.

Michael H. Hanson
Piscataway, NJ
Autumn 2017

CHAPTER ONE

Romance

A Song

Your eyes are the notes of a song, born of finely lilting meter, and precision, and rhythmic perfection.

Your laughter, silver, the words of a song, joyous lyric, and script, chiseled into polished eternity.

Your smile is the unity of a song, made harmony, and melody, in lush full lullaby.

Your heart. Your wonderful vibrant glowing heart, is an orchestra and choir made whole upon the unmatched opus of your glorious beauty.

And I play you, and sing you, sweet draught of ecstasy, upon the strings of my soul and the keys of my spirit in awed enraptured unfettered adoration.

One perfect chord,
of resonant,
and undying,
LOVE.

Cryptically Hip

She dances far outside my real
amidst the shades of cooler trees,
ethereal with raw repeal,
beyond my grasp and lesser needs.

A charmed enigma in my dreams,
Bohemian in voice and thought.
a canvas rich with twilight creeds
sweet lissome siren I once sought.

Utopian in grace and form,
both fanciful and packed with zeal,
her will a strangely hidden storm
unfettered by my pale appeal.

This weak confession from my lips,
this kitschy, post-modern worship,
most chic of all nonchalant chicks,
This goddess, cryptically hip.

On A Golden Shore*

She moves in Beauty, like a sea
of breathing green and azure sighs,
this lovely mermaid from the deep
whose amber tresses and doe eyes
go peaceful to that gentle glee
which majesty rarely denies.

On golden shores her ancient dance
of muted move and precious pose
enjoins as love and soul enhance
anointed hands in sweet repose
expressing moments burned in chance
where all of form and rhythm flows.

'Pon haunted knee and sculptured thigh
unspoken whispers genuflect
in shades of passion still and shy
serenity and soul reflect
a silken neck and perfect line,
the purity of self respect.

Thus slowing wave, and inner light
and tears of oceanic grace
soon bathe in rivers far from sight
within her tender blushing face
'neath sun ablaze and blinding bright
revealing virtue true and chaste.

At Summer's end her limbs express
a grace, a sweep, so innocent

and joy that frees me to confess
this fable of sheer sentiment
unto a heart adorned and blest
and gaze divinely eloquent.

*With due respect to the poetic works of Lord George Gordon Byron

On Errant Days

On errant days she whispers pleas
and prays for fortune's sweet bequest
yet hears, just silence, on her knees
and loneliness within her breast.

On errant days she dreams of knights
most dashing, resolute, and brave
who storm the castle of her frights
and mounted spirit her away.

On errant days she ponders fate
and all wonders that time denies
and curses history's estate
whose promises are gilded lies.

She is the soul of womankind
with sufferings, sadly sublime.
One errant day her lot will shine
and on that day I'll make her mine.

Conqueror Kiss (she said)

You have captured my heart, fine sir,

with your smile thus cast from within
your dalliance, most unaware
as you stride across my vision's stage
alight, and bright, and most debonair.

You have snared my soul, dear man,
and joyous rogue with errant wisps
of cast-off manly charms upon the wind
as your rich cerulean eyes shine
above your sweet captivating grin.

You have woven dreams, my Love,
in your tapestry and lyrics sown
upon my dark fertile loneliness
blessing me with nocturnal wishes
and conquering me with but a kiss.

Remember

I still remember her green eyes
that shined so very poignantly
amidst soft pale and tender sighs
and warm, impassioned dallying.

I still remember her sweet smile
whose timid welcoming allure
could tame a heart unduly wild
with gifts both radiant and pure.

I still remember her soft kiss
thus granted on the midnight hour,
a draught of rich heavenly bliss,
an intertwined angelic bower.

Her beauty haunts my memory
until the dawn awakens me,
and so, we end, this shadowed tryst
of mortal man and Will o' Wisp.

Harbor Deck

A summer day. Noon. Standing on that beach house deck. The inner harbor. Audience to resting sailboats, swimmers, and dog walkers.

Talking. Laughing. Newly introduced. You speak of art, show me turpentine, and painter's knife, how artists make their will apparent upon small square canvases.

Your presence glows, your smile a beacon, introducing me to shadow, and light, how one sees the world in its truest colors. You spin magic with palette, and brush, defining intent, delicate strokes of bright multi-hued oils.

I fall, helpless, into the gentle rhythms of your sweet voice. Tides rise. Skin bakes. Seagulls scream. Afternoon wanes.

Our once-clean hands freckle in rainbow pigments, and SUPPER is finally yelled.

You leave to wash up.

My one and only art lesson reaches its lonely end.

First Kiss

I sit and contemplate my life,
a haunting archeology
and scavenge through a tomb most rife
with distant buried memories.

I feel my very mind now drift
unto the farthest shores of time
where I received a precious gift,
replying in most fervent kind.

The awkwardness of flesh on flesh,
exotic tangs and secret tastes,
a pounding deep within my chest,
the joy of youth's aggressive haste.

I dream of that enduring bliss
that sweet and magical first kiss.

Chance Met in Maryland

Thus was I invited to an evening party deep in the Maryland wood, held within the main house built of sturdy oak walls which rose to tall yet humble ceilings. The living room of the home of a celebrated master artist.

Wine and spirits flowed freely, and my ears were flooded with the iridescent language of art; and smiles like floating candlelight flickered about me, and I wandered, nodded, and laughed.

While crossing this ocean of flesh, I met the current of her dark eyes, and in a moment was held fast, anchored by my failing will to that corner of the room beside a humble fireplace whose glow was no less enchanting.

And so, I swayed to her beauty's wake, the calm harbor of her smile, cascading chestnut hair, a dream of form and movement. I struggled for stability and direction, a flimsy raft to her wiles and charms.

Then the moment broke, and I once again stood within the still center, so strangely calm, and quiet, and alone.

Summer's End

At summer's end, he bows his head
accepting nature's finite song,
and all those joys no longer fed
now wake to a dark hungry dawn.

At summer's end, she breathes a sigh
releasing her slow fading dream
of midnight walks 'neath moonlit sky
and passion's sensuality.

At summer's end, they share a kiss –
a most profound and sad embrace –
which marks the tragic death of bliss
and birth of autumn's haunting grace.

And so it is that hearts may mend
a crippling wound at summer's end.

Candy Girl

I work beside this confectionary dish
a petite sweet, with eyes like licorice.

Her smile makes this little boy say yum,
her breath the rum of bubble gum.

But it ain't funny, my bit-o-honey
I crave like Goodtime's chocolate bunny.

This neat carbohydrate treats in a wrap
withholding her unfolding
from this cold vanilla Frap.

So I give Jack Daniels' lollypops the lick
and drink hot shots of peppermint schnapps
and Godiva-spiked chocolate Nestles Quik

Candy's dandy.
Liquor's quicker.

A Meal

He prepares a meal, for her, his darling
with warming expectations of a dream
in his simple solitary kitchen
after washing hands in a mountain stream.

He kneads bread dough with slow gentle squeezes,
cuts vegetables with an ancient knife.
Crushes rosemary, grinds black pepper and
spritzes olive oil 'til the fish is right.

He anoints his modest table with clean,
fraying linen, candles of gold bee's wax,
a plate of cold, salty Amish butter,
decanted wine in an etched crystal flask.

He ties back white floral-patterned curtains,
raises the shades and opens up the blinds
and an auburn sunbeam blesses this meal
most redolent in lavender and chive.

He waits for her on the front porch wiping
hot virgin crumbs off of his blue jeaned thigh
and basks in quiet anticipation
of one perfect tranquil evening in time.

First Tryst

The fumbling awkwardness of sin,
intoxicating radiance,
the drive of hot adrenaline,
the bane of inexperience.

The heat and spark of shared desire
igniting passion's very blood,
a holocaust of sensual fire,
a boiling unstoppable flood.

Insanity without control
this madness of eternity,
an aftermath of mingled souls
adrift within infinity.

Beyond all rationality
life's dark and sweetest mystery.

Autumn's Kiss

The breath of autumn welcomes me
with cool and lissome whispering
that falls across each gentle leaf
and sets my lips to whistling.

We walk along a forest path
which winds around a lovely knoll –
a musky, pungent, floral bath,
a drink that purifies my soul.

She circles with bewitching grace
adorned in nature's gaudy dress
and offers up a gorgeous face
that pledges peaceful, charming rest.

Thus, I am granted my last wish,
embraced in autumn's luscious kiss.

Valentine

I pray believe a gentle thought
engendering a pleasant whim,
this gesture unexpectedly wrought,
this kiss upon your dimpled chin.

I pray believe a tender word
expressing joyful inner glee
to have one's very feelings heard
upon this day so joyfully.

Such honeyed moments can't be wrong ,
such births within a heart sublime,
this distant sweet impassioned song
that bids you well, sweet Valentine.

Rain

I knew a girl when I was young
whose hippie parents dubbed her Rain
and like her name her raven hair
cascaded down with dark disdain
defying common gravity
her sable strands would never fain
submit to comb or cute barrette
a sweet medusa none could tame
and so I came to love this girl
when we both became of an age
where urgency routs sanity
and amber locks met ebon mane,
too soon our ardor was forbade
her parents bade and moved away.

For years I've felt a dwindling rage
not quite faded turn to jaded
dreams haunting me in middle-age.

First Love

And our entire world is born
made whole upon the very strength
of our attraction's every morn
that wakes in loving sweet embrace.

Twin torsos hot electric beat
'tween moments of eternal peace
in raptured joyous harmony
and cries of passion's fierce release.

Oh gloried stretch of Autumn days
inert to coming Winter's chill
most unaware of future pains
and blatant signs portending ill.

Three months, and then, this angel left
my ravaged heart, and soul, bereft.

Strangers With Names

Strangers with names and civilized manners
they shared an afternoon of adventure,
not colleagues, but growing familiars
window shopping and sipping fruit smoothies.

They met through common humble circumstance
connecting by mutual dalliance
thus fate introduced him to her brown eyes
and he fell, entangled, within her spell.

Sweet auburn summer light fell on the day
while he watched her walking away,
so poised, so elegant with charming composure,
a precious dream reaching its waking end.

Weekend passed and he left that cape island
pining over the memory of her.
Now he writes his passive-aggressive poems
that slowly boldly whisper, I love you.

Pen Pals

Across the waves of time we've talked
and shared our dreams and wants
reliving tales of life and love
adventures, journeys, jaunts.

And in your words I've seen a face
a gentle trusting girl
whose tender smiles and timid eyes
have set men's hearts awhirl.

And knowing that we're far away
a continent apart
I know that I am truly safe
from my own selfish heart.

For we are friends within our words
which bind us like a book
and gives us strength and honesty
against which Gods have shook.

And pondering eternity
and these few words I've sent
remember me in future days
and this pale blandishment.

Unrequited

To never love creates a curse
upon a nobly humbled home
whose silent beds remain averse
to raucously pedantic poem.

To never love predicts a crime
whose end is writ on prison walls
by wraiths who spend their Christmastime
exchanging looks down childless halls.

To never love makes bright the shame
of one whose dull and listless soul
would revel in a pauper's claim
that others' passions pay his toll.

In short, my heart is like a room
whose light may enter from above;
but curtains keep this room in gloom
of one whose heart may never love.

Last Time

Last time I saw you walk away,
your flesh was bathed in blue moonlight
and wearing my fatigues your sway
held all the lustiness of night.

Last time we danced it was midnight
without our shirts and chest to chest
and grooving to Gerald Albright
kissing his sax like a firm breast.

Last time we talked you would not turn
around and look me in the eyes
and with a guileless, soulless spurn
you left me for a cold sunrise.

Memories are all I have left
of your sweet azure silhouette.

An Evening Shore

Would you wait upon an evening shore
anticipating that first sight of me
approaching like some prince from timeless yore --
aspect of brave, gentle nobility?

Would passion brace the patience of your heart
and grant me moments of eternity
to cross this harsh gap like some mythic dart,
collapsing breathless with forehead to knee?

Could you accept one who humbly worships
with words of frank and tender sentiment ,
that bridge and join our dry and thirsty lips
beneath this dusk star's blushing sacrament?

Enjoined, entwined, and intermingling cries;
hammers in my heart, sweet fires in your eyes.

The Bread of Her Smile

Her very presence is a fine banquet,
she nourishes the emptiness in me,
joyous horns of plenty blossom from her,
truly she is the Goddess of Repast.

A harsh hunger cries out within my soul
a loneliness of weakness and despair.
My mouth waters in anticipation
of this pious, sensual Eucharist.

Her haunting eyes are the spice of beauty,
I drink the wine of her honeyed laughter.
A pauper, I worship at her table
and I feast upon the bread of her smile.

I Remember Her Kiss

I remember her kiss
that glorious tickle
of rich soaking pressure
and flowery caress
with its smooth, warm sweetness,
lightning dance between tongues,
a giving and taking,
a sharing and bonding,
joined gentle surrender,
a sighing, a dying
and raw rampaging
wet moment.
Peaceful bliss.
I remember her kiss.

Perhaps One Day

My longing for you continues to grow,
Unhampered by distance and passing time,
And perhaps one day I will tell you so.

On that morning we met, how could I know,
Your shy loveliness would curse me to pine?
My longing for you continues to grow.

Look now, and see, what your beauty has sown
A deeply rooted most passionate vine,
And mayhaps one day I will tell you so.

The absence of your smile should bring me low,
My memory drinks it, the sweetest wine.
My longing for you continues to grow.

My inner conviction wills me to show,
you a most humble, confessional sign,
And perchance one day I will tell you so.

But for now this cowardice is my foe
An un-scalable mountain I would climb.
Thus all my longings continue to grow,
And I pray one day I can tell you so.

Supercollider

Each of us is a super collider,
a complex and gargantuan engine
arcanely generating torturous
accelerations of hurt and regret.

Feelings, wounds that move at the speed of thought
through labyrinthine tunnels in our souls;
sufferings that build fatal momentum,
circling to an inevitable crash.

But there are also particles of joy,
fragments of beauty and atoms of trust;
the physics of mutual attraction
when two hearts collide in a burst of love.

Chapter Two
Introspection

Jubilant Whispers

In my childhood I hid, shaking, behind my mother's skirts, petrified by the world, a cowering soul, a cowardly mole, safe and secure deep inside of myself.

In my teenage years I bloomed, awkwardly stripping off coats of content baby fat, unnerved by the appeal of the fair sex and desperate to shed my father's chains.

In my twenties I embraced the college scene, the vibrant classes, the joy of beer, that sweet thrill of guerilla filmmaking, and the paradise, and crush, of first love.

In my thirties I took to married life, a five-day work week, buying a house, doing yard work, small talk with my neighbors, watching it decay to fated divorce.

Now in my forties I am cocooning myself in poetry spun daily on my computer screen, humble confessions, lasting desires, and flickers of dim hope.

I feel a pressure building inside me,
an explosion of jubilant whispers.

Haunted

I'm haunted by my failing dreams
and all my petty fantasies
of fateful journeys, loves, and deeds
which cower like lost refugees.

I'm haunted by ambition's plea
to pen a noble righteous tale;
to write my generation's creed --
a flawless tome none could assail.

I'm haunted by my smitten heart
whose walls were breached with errant ease
by sweet infatuation's dart
and dark obsession's mortal need.

I'm haunted by my cowardice
which hides behind my every wish;
while ghosts of every earthly dread
now taunt and fester in my bed.

Fading

I raise a crass ceramic stein
and toast the sleeper in my soul
who dreams of quaffing passion's wine
and Autumn tryst and woodland stroll.

Impersonal this cycled bite,
this endless Sisyphusian chore,
this senseless repetitious rite
and empty daily hollow horror.

My spirit rails against my ribs
demanding promised sustenance
so long denied beneath the fibs
of future raise and providence.

Each day a weaker shallow breath
this bane of incremental death.

Forward

I ponder that which I have lost
across the depth and span of time
as all my limitations pause
examining this dread decline.

The frankness of a morning run,
the ease of gait, and stride, and sprint,
the joy of burning heart and lung,
the pride of hard exertion spent.

I walk on this macabre machine
no longer spry and blithely lithe
and chase pathetic hope and dream
to capture youth's enduring jibe.

I blunder on and rally rage
defiant in my mortal cage.

I Wanted

I wanted to be like Kwai Chang Kane, a Master of Kung Fu, traveling barefoot across the American old west, immune to the elements, at peace with the world, stomping Caucasian rednecks into the dirt with artistic moves of my hands and feet, using Crane Style and Tiger and Dragon, but always acting humble, right, I can't forget that...

I wanted to be like Robin the Boy Wonder and have a really cool legal guardian who was rich and I was his ward and we would have secret identities and ride around in a rad black car and together, and we would rumble with bad guys and punch out their lights and we would wear really neat masks and capes...

I wanted to be like INS Reporter Karl Kolchak, The Night Stalker, tracking down weird creatures and monsters and strange things in the night and always defeat them with my wits, or better yet, through sheer dumb luck...

I wanted to be like Spock the Vulcan science officer on the Starship Enterprise, taller than the Captain, always laid back, unaffected by hurtful emotions with an extra long life-span, three times as strong as a human with super hearing and an enlarged neo-cortex which gave me superior analytical abilities...

I wanted to be like Steve Austin, The Bionic Man, a former Astronaut barely alive who got bionic replacements for his right arm, right eye, and both legs, and I would be stronger than anyone else and leap the highest fences and run as fast as a speeding car though I could only accomplish such feats in slow motion...

I wanted all of these things.

But then I grew up, and all that I got, was me.

I Guess

I guess I'm one of many souls
so disconnected from the world
my sad and weathered blue portals
are blind to every tempting pearl.

I guess I am a sorry sight,
misshapen in both heart and mind
all bent within from petty blight
that springs from fiddling shameful crime.

I guess I am a bitter fool
aware of my offensive flaws,
each one a horrid uncut jewel
whose imperfection claws and gnaws.

Pale veins invade my golden crown
and treasured flesh will slowly fade.
Despair has left my spirit bound --
imprisoned in this royal cave.

Is It?

Is it too late to rise anew
and dare to face a brilliant dawn
and breathe in the world's charming bloom
and free my heart from its dark bond?

Is it too late to tender bliss
upon a damsel I hold dear
and feed her lips a gentle kiss
and wash away her every tear?

Is it too late to have a life
and all the hopes that wishes bring
and stride in pride through daily strife
and smile, and laugh, and love, and sing?

This urgent plea, I shout, on high
beneath a grey unfeeling sky.

Lifeline

I read your words, my longtime friend
which gently flow across my screen
and promise that my heart will mend
and once again fulfill my need.

I read your words, which tender hope
and echo from your humble guile
the strength of your kind safety rope
and comfort of your comely smile.

I read your words, from far away
this letter from a distant shore,
this priceless gift that will not fade
when passing through my rural door.

And as your spirit fills my gaze
it whispers dreams of brighter days.

Dreams and Fates

In the one hand are all my dreams,
the other, fate.
From sleeping lands that I have seen
I choose the joy of blessed dreams.
Though pondering the world of late,
I feel the pull of waking life
whose noble cause engenders fate
to battle strife
and war on hate.

My soul is wedded to my dreams,
and heart to fate.
Rejecting all life's agonies
my spirit favors lovely dreams.
But then my heart feels evil's mate,
whose loathsome wretched horrid bite
so stirs the hunger of my fate
I prey on spite
and ravage hate.

And so I bid farewell to dreams,
and greet my fate.
Though sleeping realms are quite serene
we are not meant for lotus dreams.
There is a world we can create
with humble hands and renewed sight,
endowing paths to all our fate
with gentle light
that splinters hate.

Elegiac Apparel

I know a man who wears regrets
like existential hand-me-downs
clothing his shame from cabinets
packed with a life's winces and frowns.

He dresses each and every morn
in tailored suits of second thoughts,
his breast pocket stuffed with a scorn
and constant doubts his fitted socks.

His tie is a vain hangman's noose
offered up to all passing maids
and his glistening, ebony shoes
he walks on like the sharpest blades.

Draped in a self-fulfilling hell
alas I know him all too well.

Brother's Child

I look upon my brother's child
and see the face of distant life,
the echoed breath of ancient trial,
inherited and sorrowed strife.

I see a trail of wandering
and desert caravans anon,
I see existence prospering
always traveling on and on.

This child's endearing smiles endure,
one part of this unending dream,
a song of wisdom true and pure
a hope passed through eternity.

This blest unbroken memory
and testament to destiny.

Fragmenting

How ordinary, and how commonplace
these plain and miniscule covalent bonds
that shape reality, our existence;
make us solid, and singularly whole.

What comprises life's simple unsung glues?
Joy of parent and child, sweet cherished hugs;
loving spousal kisses, sibling laughter --
harmonic strings that twine the heart and soul.

And when these covenants disintegrate --
death, divorce, or simple relocation;
the matrix of human spirit unspools --
a slow chain-reaction of ruptured hope.

Thus, loneliness is made fissionable;
our very essence begins...fragmenting.

Goodbye

Goodbyes are like a fragile jewel
too oft displaying nervous knee
which marks a moment strangely ruled
by formal quaint civility.

And in these strange and structured airs
a most important hope is lost,
that all our common dreams and cares
will be the proper mannered cost.

So take a care to ponder well
the balance that your life has run
and pray express your best farewell
so that it is a lasting one.

And do not leave here sad or grim
for change is life's most constant peer
and visions of mutual whim
will comfort you each passing year.

If I

If I escaped these crippling walls
of haunting insecurity
would you accept my timid galls
and listen to my tender plea?

If I revealed my inner truth
bared helpless 'neath an Autumn sky
would you accept this humble proof
that my respect is not a lie?

If I approached you for awhile
no longer circling Widdershin
would you accept my gentle smile
and trust me as your paladin?

My heart would sing triumphantly
if your sweet eyes but noticed me.

What She Sees

Beneath the stars she'll oft reflect
beside a gentle sleeping sea
with flowing hair 'pon silken neck
and all her dreams a mystery.

Well mirrored in each tender eye
the grace of Heaven's majesty,
this spectacle of jeweled sky
and wondrous cosmic symphony.

How glorious must be each thought
beyond this crude hyperbole
a treasure trove we all have sought
a realm of sheer serenity.

The radiance of what she'll see.
Sweet moments in eternity.

In Sleep

In sleep, my troubles fade away
undressed in naked eloquence
where all my fears are led astray
and all my hopes grow radiant.

In sleep, I conquer every task
and stumble not while journeying
and no one sees beneath the mask
of my obsessive worrying.

In sleep, I'm granted every wish
and lack for neither friend nor love
and wallow in most selfish bliss
as sacred songs rain from above.

Through sweet eternity I roam
until I wake up all alone.

Does Anybody

Does anybody see my tears
that bleed from cuts of bitter grief,
a horrid pulse of salty jeers
that scurry like a fleeing thief?

Does anybody hear my heart,
a savage howling wounded beast,
a demon nearly torn apart,
in love's devouring selfish feast?

Does anybody feel my soul
that writhes within a raging fire
of burning lust and breathing coal
that houses all my fierce desire?

Unthinkable that none now know
my sufferings and hellish woe;
the spectacle of fiddling shames
that ravages inside my veins.

Adrift

I'm cut adrift, beyond my fears --
no longer tethered to these worlds
where all my bitter angry tears
lie strewn like lost forgotten pearls.

I'm cut adrift, thus freed of chains
no longer bound by petty creed,
and all my life's enduring banes
now bleach and painlessly recede.

I'm cut adrift to roam alone,
no longer tied by sweet desire --
a skeleton of mundane bone
devoid of all erotic fire.

Adrift, I float from day to day
untouched, unhurt, and unafraid.

Homunculus

I walk through the crowded hallways of life
slightly out of step with humanity's
odd syncopated alien movement
and weirdly hypnotic exotic acts.

Sweet interaction of parent and child,
courtship protocols, impassioned lovers,
entitled rich screwing over the poor,
the horrors of physical violence.

I try to communicate my unease
with all of these strange complex rituals
but am halted by diamond barriers
of thick impenetrable terror.

And so I live in constant daily dread
that my performance will be uncovered
and my inner machinations exposed;
unmasking my fictitious existence.

King Midas's Brother

I look in the mirror and see the change,
a transmutation of grand alchemy,
pearly rivulets streaming through my crown,
lustrous, noble, precious mineral veins.

My beard, once a bright alloy of amber
and auburn flax framing both cheek and chin
now under siege by moonlit metalsmiths,
pale armies of ivory tinkerers.

Fundamental elemental weaver –
this deeper primal Dionysian spell
alters all of those I touch to witness
my slow transformation, into silver.

Burnished by time's abrasion
and polished by life's predation.

Genesis

And so it found me naked and wandering through barren valleys of shame, no longer blind to the lies and plasters of my existence which taunted me as I stumbled flailing, clawing desperately for some greater truth, and hope, but finding only dead answers penned by silent ghosts.

Why now, deep in the middle of this fractured journey was this introduction made? I do not know, but it sang to me. Songs of roaring surf; flaming mountain tops; the grief of dying gods; cyclopean forests of musky green and love as deep and moving as a summer's day or a winter's eve.

And we embraced, this passion and I; a consummation of dream and craft, a sea change, this rupture in the void, and most feral birth.

No Longer

I no longer want to feed my critics
who denounce the truth of my humble gems;
deconstructors of flowery visions
condemning the pain that bleeds from my pens.

I no longer want to be an author
pursuing a fame and glorious prize
creating a bright immortal novel
worshipped by scholars both righteous and wise.

I no longer want to be a poet
who opens his veins and pumps out his life
in unwholesome displays of sorry rhyme,
bombastic grammar, and dramatic strife.

I no longer want to be a writer –
an insecure purveyor of letters –
glorified schemer and naked dreamer,
pretentiously proud, aping my betters.

I want to climb the highest of mountains,
shouting my rage in lightning and thunder,
shaking my fist in defiance of fate,
damning my crippling fortunes asunder.

Within My Heart

Within my heart all secrets hide
Far from the truth of questing eye,
Encased in shadowed mystery,
A shy retiring refugee
Whose every single dream has died.

A prisoner of shame and pride,
Intelligent yet far from wise,
And on his bitter bed he dreams
Within my heart.

He knows the world exists outside,
A wondrous realm where lovers fly,
While troubadours sing joyously,
Despite each earthly agony,
Crippling the spirits that reside
Within my heart.

Chapter Three
The Past

When I Was Small

I remember when I was small, the first time I took our dog Rusty, a full-grown reddish-brown purebred German Dachshund (that we kids had found abandoned in the neighborhood one night), on a walk, on a metal linked leash, outside of our apartment building in the Perlacher Forest Army Housing Project in Munich, Germany. Then Rusty heard another dog in the distance, and barked, and struggled against me to chase after it, and won, pulling the leash out of my weak little hands. And my eldest siblings went out and found him. And I was not allowed to walk him again.

I remember when I was small, my older brothers would go "comic trading." They would take a small cardboard box, filled with 50 or so odd comic books, DC, Marvel, you name it, all non-sequential, and walk from door to door in all of the apartment buildings that housed military families. They would knock on each door and then say "comic trade!" And if said family had a child who owned comics, they would sit down inside on the doorway, or in the hallway, haggling over comic trades, like professional baseball card entrepreneurs. But I could not do this myself, as the box was too heavy for me to carry for more than a few feet on my own.

I remember when I was small, I went on a picnic with my eldest sister, her boyfriend, and one of my school friends. And we sat beneath the large statue of "The Mustang," the stone horse, that, along with the statue of the elephant, was one of the two mascots of the Munich American High School. And the three of them climbed up onto the back of the massive granite horse. And they encouraged me to climb up also. But each time that I would rise

up more than a foot off the ground, fear would hit me, and I shied back down, bitter, and ashamed, because it was impossibly tall and much too foreboding for me to ever conquer.

I remember when I was small, it was Christmas day. And both of my brothers and I received traditional German wood sleds (circa 1920's style) from Santa Claus. And there had been a thick snow fall the previous day. And my brothers threw on their coats, and mufflers, and mittens, and snowmobile boots, and I yelled that I wanted to go with them. And when we got outside I saw them slip their arms behind the bowed front skids of the sleds, slinging them on like backpacks. As they walked, the lower part of the sled would bounce several inches above the back of their knees. But when I tried to do this I was so short that the bottom of the sled kept bouncing against my Achilles tendons, and hurt me, and so I slowed them down, having so much trouble keeping up, complaining, whining all the way to Hospital Hill.

I remember when I was small, I spotted my two brothers get into a fight with a kid several years older (and several inches taller) than them. A bully. In moments my two fearless siblings wrestled him on the ground. I rushed to join the melee but couldn't figure out what to do. A couple of times I threw myself upon the large barbarians kicking leg. But then he would thrash it about, striking my head, or cheek, or arm, with his sneaker. And I would back off, crying, until I saw that no one was paying any attention to me and I quickly forgot my pains and jumped back in. I bit the giant twice on his big calf muscles, through his blue jeans, and that elicited wonderful glorious yelps of pain. And so this intruder eventually yelled out "uncle!" And my brothers granted their prisoner his furlough and we walked back home for supper, victors, all the while my brothers telling me, in intense and confidential voices,

"don't tell anybody we got into a fight or Dad'll kill us! You got that Mike?"

Numb

It was my third day of Kindergarten in the school at the Perlacher Forest Army Housing Project in Munich, Germany and I still found everything so very confusing and my teacher was unhappy with me because I did not know how to tie my own shoelaces and I could tell that my crayon drawings were bad because I scribbled all over the coloring book pages when everyone else carefully filled in the picture outlines.

And days earlier, I was just too young to understand the conversations of my parents about my age and whether or not 4 years and 8 months was too young for me to start school and my mother saying she needed the break for half a day as raising five kids, me the fourth of five, was overwhelming and so every morning she would stand by the curb with me and see me board the bus that would take me to school.

And each day after school, the bus would pull up beside the long three-story apartment building that I called home and I would run to the right front door, and dash up the three flights of stairs in the main stairwell and reach for the knob of the door with the seven lacquered wood name plates each one displaying the name of a member of my family in fire-branded letters, in both English and Taiwanese (we had lived near an American Army base in Taiwan a few years earlier).

And so my third day of Kindergarten came to an end and I rode the school bus back to my home and it came to a stop in my neighborhood and I stepped off the bus onto the curb and I ran to the right front door of the nearest apartment building and I flew up the stairwell, to the third floor but this time something was

wrong. The wood name-plates were not there.

And then the panic started, and I found that the door was locked. And I kicked and pounded on it and yelled "mommy!" But nothing happened. And so I ran back down the stairs. And outside. And up to the curb. And then all around myself. And I moved in a slow circle. And I saw how there were several of the large apartment buildings, which all looked exactly the same, all holding twelve apartments each, six to a stairwell. And each building had a code number on its side, and I could not remember ours.

And then I ran up the right stairwell of another building, and then another and the terror bubbled up in me, filling my stomach, and then my throat, and tears streamed down my eyes and made it difficult for me to see, and on every door where I arrived there were no wood name plates.

Finally, shattered, I found my way back to the curb where I had been dropped off and then I heard a terrible wailing voice, full of terror, and I realized it was my own voice, building with horror, screaming, one word, over and over again.

"Mommmmmyyyyyyyyy!"

And then an eternity passed, or maybe no time at all. And her arms were around me, and my red wet face smashed into her side. And she walked me to the correct apartment building, hugging me close speaking her soothing words, and sighs, and coos, those wonderful secret sounds that only a mother knows, and she sat me down on the living room couch, mute, beneath a blanket, because I shivered so. And that fear, that horrible terror that had drowned me, was now far away, and soon the shaking subsided. And I ignored my food during supper.

I didn't notice anyone around me that night. I did not hear the voices of my two brothers and my two sisters. And even my father's usual cutting baritone went unfelt, like water striking a rock.

And thus I fell into myself. A long spiraling endless drop. Down. Deep beneath the protection and safety of nothingness. A glorious wonderful absence of all.

Numb.

Family

Thus born on near and distant shore
in regimented ranks were raised
five troopers from a time of yore,
five warriors of weary gaze.

We forded Ancient Taiwan streams
and burned in Arizona's heat
and stormed Germanic castle greaves
'til our mad Sergeant met defeat.

With two red shaggy refugees
we braved a cold and northern home
and grew until we took our leave
of hearth for safe nomadic roads.

Maternal tolls, Paternal wounds,
retreating souls, outflanking dooms.

When My Brother Was Psychic

There was a time, long ago, when my brother was psychic.

He was ten years old. One of five American army brats, living in Perlacher Forest Army Housing in Munich, Germany. It was 1969. And our Father kept looking at Wayne intensely, strangely, every night during supper over the past week. Wayne laughed when Dad did this because he thought our Father was trying to be funny.

And then over the next few days Wayne overheard Dad make cryptic comments to our Mother in that resonating baritone of his.

"I think he heard me Martita. You see how he reacts? He says what is on the back of the cards! He guessed three face cards in a row! I tell you he's got the ability."

And then one weekend, on a Saturday morning without notice Dad told Wayne that the two of them were going to McGraw Kaserne, the Army Headquarters building in Munich. Wayne smiled! And left behind the jealous stares of his siblings.

And McGraw Kaserne was the coolest place. And they stepped into the neatest elevators ever, because there were no doors on them. And signs that warned you to stay behind yellow lines on the ground whenever the elevator was in motion.

And then my Father walked Wayne into a small office and up to a pleasant looking younger man dressed just like Dad. And they started talking.

"Yah, Rod?"

"Bill, I'd like to introduce you to my son. Wayne, this is Sergeant Bill Francke."

And then my Father looked at Wayne expectantly with his green hazel eyes that were the same color as Wayne's.

"Tell me. What is Sergeant Francke thinking?" Wayne lost his breath.

"It's okay Wayne. You can do it. Tell Sergeant Francke what he is thinking."

Wayne just stared at both of them in shock. Not understanding. Not getting it. Scared.

"Well, uh, it's interesting to meet you young man. If you'll excuse me Rod I have an appointment."

And the Sergeant walked away, shaking his head.

And then our Father sighed in disappointment. And took my brother to the McGraw Kaserne Servomat! The vending machine room! The coolest room in the building!

Because it had "dozens" of vending machines made of shiny glistening glass and stainless steel which sold every single kind of food and drink imaginable. Sandwiches.

Hot soup. All many of candy bars. Fresh fruit. Peanuts. Soda pop. Water. Coffee. Tea. Pizza. You name it. A modern high-tech cornucopia wondrous to behold. It was like some place out of the Jetsons, or Star Trek. And Dad bought Wayne an ice cream sandwich.

And then the two of them went back downstairs in the big elevators that had no doors and got inside our family's dull blue VW bug, and Dad turned to Wayne, and said in that pleasant baritone voice of his, "Now don't tell anyone about what happened this morning Wayne. If anyone asks, I just had to pick up some paperwork. Okay?"

And Wayne nodded his head, licking the remains of the delicious ice cream off of his lips.

And Wayne never spoke of this incident for the next twenty-five years, until the day after our Father's funeral.

And so that, dear reader, is what really happened on the other side of the Atlantic Ocean, in that long ago time, when my brother was psychic.

Wood Mosaic

It hangs on my far kitchen wall,
quaint, rustic family heirloom,
a blending of beautiful wood
and scene from a hard, simpler time.

The craftsmanship is quite subtle
this marriage of skill and folk art
created by my grandfather
within the autumn of his life.

I never knew him, cold old man --
granger, handyman, carpenter,
surly artisan in the rough.
Distant, simple North Country son.

I gaze upon his mosaic
birthed of tree trunk, chisel, and stain.
It haunts my soul, as Farmer and
horse-cart travel on, always on…

Repairman

My father, an appliance repairman, could mend the insides of things. He could ferret out hidden flaws, replace broken parts with working ones.

Looking within each washer, dryer, refrigerator, each stove, instinctively he knew the whole of them, how they bind in mechanical harmony.

But for some unfathomable reason this did not translate to flesh and bone-- the foundations of human spirit, for HE was damaged, in need of repair.

Was it an unloved, repressive childhood, or a North Korean cannon shell? Its shrapnel slaying his platoon, his buddies, blasting him out of his driver's seat and into a coma, severing his optic nerve.

Amoral liar, sexual predator, cowardly sociopath-- was it a cracked bearing in the gears of your mind, or a frayed belt upon the drum of your heart?

Repairman, why couldn't you fix your own malfunctioning soul?

Chapter Four
Nature

Solitary Spring

Alone, in Spring, when Winter dies
and one is wont to ponder life
and contemplate the changing skis
and mother earth's three months of strife.

Apart, in Spring, when snowy melt
will slake the thirst of waking plant
and fading white reveals the welt
of Autumn bruises on the land.

Forlorn, in Spring, when you're alone
and breaking bread for just one mouth
and silence echoes in your home
as joyous birds depart the south.

And on this chill of early Spring
a rain of sorrows claw and cling.

Spring Blossoms

I would take your hand on this warm Spring day, and lead you through a field of soft downy grasses. Smiling, I offer soothing sips from a carafe of golden dandelion wine. And joyously we run and shout at white-freckled cerulean skies, until finally we collapse, laughing, at the foot of the flowering Sakura tree.

I do not know who you are, and you probably don't know me, but I sense your spirit, out there, adrift, like mine, floating on the cool yet tender breeze that makes these white and pink cherry blossoms shiver, seductively, on their long delicate branches.

August Breathes

Fair August breathes a fiery laugh
and dimples on bright golden sands
a bawdy flirt across the map
sashaying through all summer lands.

The warmest smile throughout the year
a hug that welcomes one and all
most joyous kiss 'neath blue veneer
this heated tryst before the fall.

These final waves of amber love
(thus break upon a mortal shore)
whose total days count thirty one
and join those months of August yore.

This Wintertide

Angelic choirs of laughing rhyme
which giggling kids can't hold inside;
we smell the pitch of blushing pine
that snuggles us at wintertide.

Sweet crystal flakes upon our tongue,
flimsy toboggans all can ride.
We gulp hot cider like a sponge
and sculpture snow at wintertide.

The thrill of daily greeting card,
warm crushing hugs at fireside,
most loving call beckons homeward
uniting us at wintertide.

Now one score years and nine have passed
since my last family yuletide.
I reminisce a distant past
that haunts me on this wintertide.

Chapter Five

Beauty

Naked in Waves

At ease, I walk into his studio
to greet a friend I made one bygone year.
Before his palette and his canvas lies
this vision, aesthetically austere.

She floats upon a graceful green divan.
Unfashionably long and lissom hair
that spills across her breasts to slowly pool
over endless limb, neck, and hip laid bare

where poise so coy defies embarrassment;
marble visage -- in studied quiet style,
thus makes this creature's exotic features,
and darkest charms a most bewitching guile.

Enthroned, barely tolerating her slaves,
on jade majestic sea, naked in waves.

Chocolate Dancer

This elegant and lissome lass
whose every movement is a song
blossomed in Harlem's perky past,
an artist sinewy and strong.

She had graceful, finely honed hands
like butterflies adrift in air,
she pranced with feet like wind on sands
pirouetting with flash and flair.

Known as black pearl and bronze Venus,
treated unfairly on our shore
she was compelled to thus leave us
to gild another country's lore.

Mystic murmurs in all her steps
chocolate dancer, the true answer
why men worship the fairer sex.

This Maryland

It is within the trees of Maryland
where all of my dreams become one.
Where endless trails lead on and on
and grassy slopes beckon unto me
where farmer and hunter share the land
and horse and cattle graze as friends
and early bird and morning dew
greet each day from their green dens.

It is in the soul of Maryland
where all of my hopes become one.
And sunlight blankets forest scape
and walls of oak and solid stone
carve their voices 'pon the Earth
in sweet songs of life, and existence
made whole beyond the distant banks
of waters darkly ebullient

It is in the heart of Maryland
where all of my humanity becomes one.
And visiting, I reenter the world
upon a hillside, a warm farmhouse
and landscape tamed by loving hand
this home to gloried artisan
whose shadows grace a strong abode
two humble souls born of this land.

It is in the fields of Maryland
where human strife and soil became one
in conquered hill and rock and stump

and battles with thick summer air
the planting of precious life-bound seeds
of corn, soybean, wheat, and barley
and raising beasts upon such feed
cattle, sheep, and poultry.

It is in the streets of Maryland
where bustle and leisure become one
where brick and cobblestone unite
and thoroughfares and sidewalk paths
all lead down to a harbor scene
where business, travel, trade are done
the mortar of community
a wise inspired union.

It is in the rains of Maryland
where water and life become one
where river, lake, and stream delight
where beaver dams grow adamant
and rain gardens flank the urban forts
and sailboats flirt just off the shore
and swimming folk play water games
and fish and frog and snake endure.

It is in the memory of Maryland
where truth and history become one
and time gives up its mysteries
and facts surrender all their secrets
birthplace of Tubman, Douglass, Brent
the brave defense of Antietam
the doom of Edgar Allen Poe
the hunt for Lincoln's Assassin.

It is in the bosom of Maryland
where faith and religion become one
and fellowship and brotherhood
run hand in hand with sisterhood
and strong beliefs breed stronger hopes
and worship beds with noble pride
and joyful prayer resonates
and all of God and man combine.

It is in the beauty of Maryland
where loneliness and desire become one
and I stumble 'pon a woodland nymph
whose aching tender loveliness
and gorgeous saddened dark fey eyes
blind me to all sanity
and to this very day I sing
her graceful form so willowy.

And it is in the whole of Maryland
that I have come full circle
and travel back unto myself
and arrive at my own beginning
and my hubris has been extinguished
and I fall 'pon hands and knees and weep
at last accepting the haunting kiss
of nature's sweet embracing sleep.

This ancient hallowed hinterland
this loving home, this Maryland.

Into Colors

She can escape into colors
at the end of every day,
perhaps when her sad heart flutters
and her soul has nothing to say.

She can float across the rainbow,
wallowing in lovely pigments
whose secrets only she can know
as they whisper wispy figments.

She can embrace a radiance,
dappled in glorious freckles,
kaleidoscopic luminance,
shimmering before dawn heckles.

Such little bright flickering hands
willing to please all her demands.

Walls

I am surrounded by beauty:
delicate, small geometries;
gold and silver gilded-age frames --
portals to far exotic lands.

Pastel, charcoal, and oil pigments,
the epidermis of art --
these wonders of lush creation
mark the borders of my kingdom.

Magic seasons of sun, snow, leaves;
charming sirens forever posed.
They all withstand my loneliness.
I am surrounded by beauty.

Chapter Six
Whimsy

The Poet Store

Each morning I enter the poet store
to shop for a fresh, crispy metaphor,
witty breads to feed a hungry reader
and cartons of appropriate meter.

I nod and smile to my fellow shoppers
sly crafty misers hoarding their coppers
frugal consumers of forced brevity
frowning in judgment of my spending spree.

The cashier puts all my goods in a bag,
slant-rhymes, adjectives, and adverbs that lag,
bottles of whimsy, large cans of dull prose
and free-range stanzas perfumed like meadows.

Squiring these groceries back to my home
I dream of preparing a sumptuous poem.

Ego Pricing

He's got curb appeal, yes that's what she said
trying to communicate her attraction
for this simple man she would have wed
if she had been a woman of action.

She's got good bones was his very first thought
struggling to explain things beyond mere word,
unaware that he was just sought,
he would have loved her had he only heard.

But both were high-strung, uptight lookie-loos
sensitive enough to know their own wants
but lacking the heart to pay all their dues
they're left with regret that hurts as it haunts.

He's a handyman's special just living alone
she's a pale fixer-upper in a no-parking zone.

The Phelpsian Age

I watched a demigod perform tonight
competing in an ancient foreign land,
a man of most singular physical
attributes, and unnatural focus.

Athlete worship is so overrated
when measured against the social problems
of this day and age... then Mike dives like a
bolt of lightning into challenged waters

and like some otherworldly hybrid of
human flesh and aquatic juggernaut
this unrelenting missile of muscle
and bone wages maritime combat, and wins!

Unparalleled triumphant victor of
eight fiercely mythic Olympic battles.

A Poem

Every one of us is a poem,
a soft fleshy composition
conveying rich, hidden meanings
and articulated beauty.

Every one of us is a verse,
a hymn writ on parchments of skin
that whispers the sweetest of dreams
and whimsies of laughter and tears.

Every one of us is a song,
a fierce, prosaic batch of years;
a fabled, mystic lullaby
dwelling in shadowed harmonies.

Every one of us is a dance,
a cry of rhythm and movement;
joyous gesture, raw expression.
A beginning, middle, and end.

CHAPTER SEVEN

Between Days

Cusp of December

We're on the cusp of December,
so many things to remember,
too many lists that fill our fists
before sparking winter's ember.
Thanksgiving charms are fading off,
no glass of cider left to quaff,
the birds have fled much farther south
as old hugs fill memory's trough.
Darkness greets all by end of work,
a landscape both dreary and stark,
an unhappy weary commute
where doubts and dangers lay and lurk.
This twilight time that two months share
red and gold leaf, carpet beneath
the chilled perfume of crispy air.

Autumn Aches

Oh Autumn aches to hibernate
as Fall is lackluster and late,
making beds of pinecone and leaf
in this bedroom of god's estate.
She savors soporific wind
that whispers of hibernal sin
whose kisses frost every window
promising dreams of starlit kin.
Sweet dusk comes earlier each day
as skies grow more silver and gray,
infusing all with pale esprit
to greet winter's frolic and play.
Resisting sleep unto the last
as her subjects now drowse and fast.

The House Of Doze

I offer you the house of doze
filled with soft, indirect sunlight
where cool summer breezes oft blow
and late fall's chills will never bite.
In wintertime log cabin walls
hold in the warmth of fireplace
and thick blanket and woolen shawls
keep out New Year's icy embrace.
Love seats and couches fill each room,
divans lined with velvet allure
where mister sleep will gently groom
your worries into something pure.
Pleasant music from every time
flows gently into soulful suites,
charming each with a dulcet chime
and rhyme pulsing with your heartbeats.
So after every filling meal,
after the joy of companions
when dusk is near, your fading zeal
is welcome to a rest, genteel
and laced with courtly compassions
neither god nor man can repeal
inside this realm of mint and rose
proclaiming peace, the house of doze.

End

Let's end it now and forever,
each and every one of us,
ropes of violence we'll sever
as all else is most treasonous.
Together we will persevere,
standing against armies of hates,
deflecting thrusts of this vile spear
that stains souls as it denigrates.
Both women and men must join hands,
braiding strong harmonious knots,
weaving a tapestry that spans
from coast to coast in all our thoughts.
This savage battle must be won
with peace never ever undone.

The Waves of Jubilee

What happens after turkey soup,
after the last turkey sandwich,
no nutrients left to recoup
from this short-lived November niche.
What resonates after the hugs
and handshakes that mark all goodbyes,
when grand gestures condense to shrugs
after the laughter, shouts, and cries.
What follows us beyond this month
when ochre skins slowly grow pale
and winter makes us all confront
the loneliness in our souls' vale.
There is a storm we sometimes see
inside our heart, within a sea
surging in waves of jubilee
that burn away melancholy.

Before Thanksgiving

Before Thanksgiving I will dream
about the coming holiday
when silver clouds billow and teem
above the streams, forest, and clay.
Before Thanksgiving I will feel
a cooling breeze on face and ears
as long walks on bright leaves anneal
my soul to all of winter's fears.
Before Thanksgiving I will hear
the echoes of tears and laughter
that by December disappear
without a regret or answer.
Before Thanksgiving I travel
an ancient highway fast and full,
a passage to a warm castle
where love is free and life peaceful.
Thanksgiving flies on breaded wings
through gravy skies o'er pecan pies
with all feasting like queens and kings.

Suspended

She's traveling on the autumn train
between both summer and winter,
watching Fall's colors slowly drain
and musky leaves dry and splinter.
She sees that time is palpable,
moving betwixt chilly and cold,
a lush and bristling animal
too fierce and fleet to catch and hold.
She finds the ride mesmerizing,
reclining in this iron coach,
nature slyly tranquilizing
her soul before city's approach.
Suspended in bright, amber dreams
floating along twin steel streams.

Such Reverence

Yes one Sunday in November
is one day that none remember
when wallowing in autumn's fog
of soft soporific splendor.
All trees have finished shaking manes
free of yellow and crimson locks,
the feast of summer's tired remains
sharing our thoughts with set-back clocks.
The weary winds are so chilly
we excavate both scarf and glove,
lighting hearths so willy nilly
fresh smoke heckles couples in love.
These moments hold such reverence
I cannot tell the difference
between the states of wake and sleep
that both lose their significance.

Sweet November

First morning frosts of November
are the visions I remember
of silver lining everything
with slowly blooming splendor.
Bright, sparkling raw glistening skin,
a grand epidermis akin
to moonlight brushing grass and leaf,
whispering winter must begin.
Vast jeweled blanket at sunrise,
a beauty that will colonize
both car windows and wide front lawns
until the sun annuls this prize.
A short, gentle wispy white kiss
offering eyes pale blazing bliss.

November's Mist

I'm haunted by November's mist
in all its wistful, wispy charm,
caressing nature with a kiss
in arms both willowy and warm.
There is an effervescent glow
that permeates this magic month,
daily battling winter's shadow,
crawling out of its labyrinth.
This season of sleepy surrounds
engenders all four-footed folk
to grow their beards in leaps and bounds
while dancing round leaf piles that smoke.
The breath of dusk is pale crimson,
a vibrant and virile vision.

Cloaked In Autumn

Cloaked in autumn, ready to sleep
and swaying in a musky breeze
she senses winter's distant creep
that whispers of a fervent freeze.
She snuggles and embraces fall
in all its fluffy finery,
a sweet, resplendent, leaf-smoked shawl
of soporific bribery.
Her kingdom is decorated
in royal red and bright amber,
a joyous time celebrated
by subjects of this enchanter.
Soon she succumbs to drowsiness
and mid-November's blazing bliss.

Out Of Phase

She's shifting in and out of phase,
her very skin a rainbow blaze
crossing between assorted worlds
that differ in so many ways.
One is a home where she's alone,
another treats her like a drone,
one gives women no rights at all,
and one has her gracing a throne.
And yet the strangest thing of all,
she loves them equally, in thrall
to all they offer and withhold
to an odd girl's weird wherewithal
that never seems to get that old
upon the universe's wall
that never ever makes landfall.

Any Belief

She's sitting on a chair on sand,
oh so precariously posed,
held steady with a single hand
and pondering all that is closed.
This is more than new-age yoga,
less than neural philosophy,
like drinking a mocha coma
on worlds bereft of botany.
The ground beneath is unstable,
her soul shifts back and forth, gently
like she's in some ancient fable
and her heart is denied entry.
She focuses without relief
desperate to gain any belief.

Into Autumn's Heart

What's in a kiss, I cannot remember
trysts between September to November
or have you also forgot Autumn's heat,
warmth from lips to knee, spreading forever.
What is it like to be inside a kiss
full of rhythm, a paradise of bliss
floating on a sea of bubbling romance
engulfed by desire's wet, ardent abyss.
What are the glees in a kiss, sweet and tart
that ripples from your taste into your heart
like a slowly raging fire on your tongue
making you love's fresh, passionate escort.
Have you crossed life's flesh and soul barrier
making you joy's exquisite carrier.

The African Dream

Bowing her head, closing her eyes
slipping into silent safety
free from all life's deadliest lies,
a brave and beautiful lady.
Cloaked in the azure shade of night,
a camouflage of sweet blackness
that hides her from the sun's harsh light
like some transformative actress.
She hears the waking song of day,
sometimes hurtful, sometimes sublime
and feeling like fresh-sculpted clay
reluctantly begins begins her climb,
an invisible castaway
paying the price all women pay
from day-to-day, from day-to-day
never at peace, never at play...

Raising This Light

She holds the flame of self-respect,
brandishing it for all to see
a prize of purest intellect
condemning men's effrontery.
She flourishes this bold beacon,
this spark that lights a holy fire
burning off lies that once weakened
the dreams to which women aspire.
Raising this light as offering,
a brave and brazen sacrifice
to stop history's conquering
that treats a female's hope like ice.
With each grand stride, she shan't abide
unfair treatment all too frequent
dark horrors so unjustified.

Are There Answers?

What is a life well lived,
in prison it's not getting shivved,
feeling safe as a kid
or embracing all that's forbid?
What's the purpose of life,
is it growing old without strife,
laughing, playing the fife
or battling nature and wildlife?
What is our destiny,
to be unbound and always free
of all hungers and need
and everything that makes us bleed?
Are there answers to these riddles
not couched in vague, arcane symbols
reduced to insults and quibbles.

The Vernis Layer

What lies beneath the Vernis layer,
that barrier across our lives
that answers neither plead nor prayer
and makes sure that our soul survives.
What pounds below this shiny crust
with fists of aching repression
and all of desire's nascent lust
that grants a heart grand ascension.
What claws at our precious veneers,
seeking to crack this amber shield
that stills our voice, closes our ears
and thus will never ever yield.
We're much more than this perfection
of flesh and mind's intersection.

Spicy Juice

Bogarting that small cigarette
this sweet, diminutive Babette,
a student of eclectic life
who never dated one regret.
Her brain is soaked in poetry
writ in the nineteenth century
she despises all politics,
favoring art's obscenity.
Bored of conventionality
and truth's sleepy banality,
desiring all that's passionate,
beyond mortal morality.
She has no time for the inane,
a spicy juice, funky and loose,
mutely condemning the mundane.

Happy Today

She is happy today, really,
a jar of glowing azure joy
with a smile, daring and silly
and eyes irresistibly coy.
She is happy today, unlike
other days in previous weeks
when dolefulness pierced like a spike
as tears ran down both of her cheeks
She is happy today, because
she earned it, yes, she really did,
she overcame all of her flaws
and embraced all that fate forbid
without, even, a single pause
and now she dances like a kid.
She's chosen to embrace her life
rejecting fear and all despair
to climb from karma's pit of strife.

Earth And Rain

The earth is humbled after rain,
after nestling a supple swain
whose kisses are overwhelming,
freckling a body without shame.
After first rain are earthy sighs
after a series of sweet cries
eclipsing a romantic pause
as daylight grows and rainstorm dies.
The rain's attraction is not sought
and it is neither sold nor bought
but freely given to the earth,
dancing about then coyly caught.
Infusing one another's grace
feeding upon each other's space
the earth receives, the rain believes
the holiness of this embrace.

A Sword

She is a sword in soul and form,
lovely, and long, and luminous
with the potential of a storm
empty of any ruefulness.
She is a blade in heart and mind,
two piercing eyes and quick to draw
a fast attack with skill refined
beyond the chains of earthly law.
She is a weapon forged and true,
hardened against petty language,
tempered for any ballyhoo
that wrongly offers her anguish.
Like steel she displays no weakness
vision of unsheathed completeness.

The Secret Rhyme

She's searching for the secret rhyme,
sifting through every clue or sign
throughout the length of her short life,
splashing about history's brine.
This rhyme existed long ago,
back when man talked with deer and crow
before Homer trod ancient Greece
and language danced a fiery glow.
Wise men whisper this hidden rhyme
was long forgotten over time,
an arcane, mystic mix of words
whose sound is both sweet and sublime.
Sometimes she thinks she feels it near
on winter nights cold and austere
or on the breath of some odd breeze
bleeding from dusk's amber veneer.
She fears it may not be intact,
this eerie verbal artifact
so perfect it offended God
the first time spoke by one enrapt.
She thinks it is a living thing
teasing as sleep begins to cling
and close her eyes before she'll hear
this miracle begin to sing.
Perhaps this rhyme might be too pure
to heed by none but a savior.

Two Flowers

Two flowers can make one bouquet,
two blossoms born of one sunbeam,
two dancers within one ballet
color my nights a lovely dream.
Two visages of bright beauty,
twins no mortal man can deny,
spreading perfumes full and fruity,
swaying to nature's sweet war cry.
Two visions sharing one witness,
one soul that shudders in delight
for something dark and delicious,
a kindred heart and worthy knight.
One cannot but bow to these jewels
taking a chance to hold this glance
forsaking life's forbidden rules.

Unbroken

Most see her broken in defeat
hobbling sadly on the sidewalk,
blind to the fact her souls complete,
a hale spirit that none can block.
She strides the street of bandages
littered with piles of broken casts
shed by victims of ravages
that condemn humanity's pasts.
Her dreams so thin she's hard to see
clothed by hard won integrity,
she is much stronger than she looks
and wears her hopes triumphantly.
Her suffering is dutiful
her heart both bold and beautiful.

Summer Angel

The summer angel is leaving,
saying goodbye to golden shore,
visage betraying deep grieving
with ocean eyes salty and sore.
She sighs and then laments the loss
of lovers walking on the beach,
laughing, drinking romance's sauce
and bedtime whispers before sleep.
She nods farewell to family fun,
picnics and bathing in the sun,
building sand castles until dusk
when all the sunbeams have unspun.
She hears Fall's song as autumn nears
then spreads her wings and disappears.

Lightning's Blink

One blink after the lightning strike,
half one heartbeat before the next
came one vision strangely dreamlike
that left my heart and soul perplexed.
In one more blink she drew nearer,
announced by one bright lightning flash,
silhouette in my eyes' mirror
accompanied by thunder's crash.
In the third blink she hovered close,
her visage supernatural,
naked, bereft of any clothes,
a goddess both fey and feral.
One last lightning bolt and she fled
as my emptiness slowly spread.

September's Sauce

September's here, Autumn is near
as rain replaces warm sunbeams,
a pure and precious time of year
as dusk retreats for early dreams.
September welcomes everyone
as harvests send their last farewells,
mittens and touks are knit and spun
while old man winter casts his spells.
September presses juicy grapes,
groaning children return to schools,
early shadows project strange shapes
predicting Fall's shower of jewels.
September's sauce placates the loss
of summer's sadly dying gloss.

Summer Leaves

Summer is leaving too quickly,
its petals slowly mummified,
a tragic change that quietly
chooses autumn to be our bride.
Summer is losing its veneer,
departing with a morning chill,
an end that's drawing ever near,
saying goodbye to warm good will.
Summer is taking its last breath,
its golden voice a fading song,
a sad farewell and humble death
for one whose life we can't prolong.
Fall greets us with a daring kiss
and harvest of chromatic bliss.

After The Burglary

Not long after the burglary,
not long after the invasion
she ponders anonymity
and her responsibility.
She thinks about a rash foot chase
that has her online friends upset,
a thought she chose not to embrace
regardless of inherent threat.
Her thoughts are shouts inside her head
yelling and screaming out in strife
that she must contemplate, unsaid,
the value of her human life.
She opts to share this happening
as her fears have gone travelling.

'Neath Shadow Bars

Thinking her way out of this place,
yes that's her intuitive plan,
first keeping quiet in this space
when all she wants is to scream damn.
She's contemplating a break-in,
planning a cognitive escape,
trying to deal with a vile sin
that's left her hurt on fate's landscape.
Her inner self just won't speak up,
it won't take her seriously,
refusing to share life's dark cup
as her heart pounds furiously.
Ready to make this inner change
'neath shadow bars and distant stars
that strangely stay just out of range.

About the Poet

Michael H. Hanson has written four collections of poetry: *Autumn Blush* and *Jubilant Whispers* whose second editions will soon be published by Racket River Press (an imprint of Copper Dog Publishing LLC), *Dark Parchments: Midnight Curses and Verses* published by MoonDream Press (an imprint of Copper Dog Publishing LLC), and *When The Night Owl Screams* also published by MoonDream Press. He has written and sold over two dozen individual poems to various periodicals, magazines, anthologies, and online venues over the past fifteen years.

Michael is the Creator of the Sha'Daa shared-world action/fantasy anthology series currently consisting of *Sha'Daa: Tales of The Apocalypse, Sha'Daa: Last Call, Sha'Daa: Pawns, Sha'Daa: Facets, Sha'Daa: Inked,* and the soon to be released *Sha'Daa: Toys* all published by MoonDream Press.

www.ingramcontent.com/pod-product-compliance
Lightning Source LLC
Chambersburg PA
CBHW070642050426
42451CB00008B/266